Who Is
Carol Burnett?

by David Stabler

illustrated by Robert Squier

Penguin Workshop

For my mom—RS

PENGUIN WORKSHOP
An imprint of Penguin Random House LLC
1745 Broadway, New York, New York 10019

First published in the United States of America by Penguin Workshop,
an imprint of Penguin Random House LLC, 2025

Visit us online at penguinrandomhouse.com.

Library of Congress Cataloging-in-Publication Data is available.

Printed in the United States of America

ISBN 9780593886564 (paperback)   10 9 8 7 6 5 4 3 2 1 CJKW
ISBN 9780593886571 (library binding)   10 9 8 7 6 5 4 3 2 1 CJKW

Contents

Who Is Carol Burnett?

On September 11, 1967, just before 10:00 p.m., thirty-four-year-old Carol Burnett gathered around the television set with her family in their Los Angeles living room. Together with her husband, Joe, she settled in to watch her brand-new TV series, *The Carol Burnett Show*.

There were potato chips and popcorn on the coffee table, but Carol was too nervous to eat.

Though she had been an actress and comedian for more than ten years, Carol had never had her own TV show before. She was terrified that no one would like it.

On the screen, Carol walked out onto a stage wearing a yellow polka-dot dress. Her bright red hair was cut short. She introduced herself and answered questions from the audience. After the musical theme played, a series of comedy skits and songs began. Though Carol had taped her first show some weeks earlier, this was her first time watching it. She spent the entire hour peeking through her fingers at the TV.

When it was over, the "good night" music played. All the members of the cast gathered onstage to sign their names in Carol's scrapbook. Guest star Jim Nabors signed first, followed by funnyman Harvey Korman. Actress and comedian Vicki Lawrence added her signature, and then tall, handsome Lyle Waggoner.

The credits rolled. Watching at home, Carol breathed a sigh of relief. She had done it. The live audience had laughed all the way through. Most importantly, her family loved it. Now she just had to hope that TV viewers across the country would like it, too.

Over the next week, Carol began to sense that her new show was a hit. Fan letters started arriving at the studio: one hundred, then two hundred.

Vicki, Harvey, and Lyle received fan mail, too. By the middle of November, forty stations in the United States were showing *The Carol Burnett Show* on Monday nights. As the first woman to host her own TV variety show, Carol had made history.

How did a shy red-haired girl from Texas grow up to be one of America's most popular television stars? It wasn't easy. Raised by her grandmother, Carol forged her own path from San Antonio to Hollywood to Broadway and beyond. And she did it all while overcoming obstacles that would have stopped most people in their tracks. Her inspiring success story proves that happy endings really do happen.

CHAPTER 1
Hollywood Kid

Carol Creighton Burnett was born on April 26, 1933, in San Antonio, Texas. Her father, Joseph, managed a movie theater there. Her mother, Ina, was an avid movie fan. She named Carol after one of her favorite film stars, actress Carole Lombard.

Carol grew up in the early days of the economic crisis known as the Great Depression. Though her father had a steady job, he often struggled to provide for the family. He turned to alcohol to deal with the stress of putting food on the table. Carol's mother also started drinking. In time, they both became addicted to alcohol. When they drank, they argued a lot.

When Carol was seven years old, her parents moved to California in search of a better life. But their arguments continued. Eventually, they separated, leaving Carol in the care of her mother's mother, Mabel "Mae" Eudora White, whom she called Nanny. Carol and Nanny lived in a small, cramped boarding house in Hollywood, the home of the movie industry. (A boarding house is a home where guests rent rooms and have their meals together.) Nanny worked nights as a cleaning woman at a movie studio to pay the bills.

Carol's mother lived close by and visited them often. Carol's father lived with his own mother in nearby Santa Monica.

As a child, Carol developed the same love of movies that her mother had. Her favorite movie was *Pinocchio*. Her favorite stars included Barbara Stanwyck, Joan Crawford, and her namesake,

Carole Lombard. To pay for tickets, Carol collected glass milk and soda bottles and turned them in for the deposit money. She went to the movies at least five times a week! Sometimes she even sneaked a roll or two of toilet paper from the theater bathroom to bring home to her family.

When Carol was nine, she started to do a "Tarzan yell" in imitation of the big-screen jungle hero played by Johnny Weissmuller. Johnny starred in twelve *Tarzan* movies between 1932 and 1948.

When she was in second grade, Carol invented an imaginary twin sister whom she called Karen. Karen had dimpled cheeks like the popular child actress Shirley Temple. When she was feeling especially mischievous, Carol dressed up as "Karen" and tried to fool her neighbors in the boarding house. When Carol was tired, Karen mysteriously vanished. In 1944, when Carol was eleven, her mother gave birth to a baby girl, Chrissie. Now Carol had a real-life half sister who came to live in the boarding house with her and Nanny.

Carol (right) and her half sister, Chrissie

The Golden Age of Hollywood

"The golden age of Hollywood" is a term used to describe a period in the history of American movies from the late 1920s to the early 1960s. During these years, five film studios—MGM, Paramount, Fox, Warner Bros., and RKO—made almost all the movies released in the United States.

The two decades of the 1930s and '40s, in particular, produced some of the most popular movie stars of all time, including Clark Gable and Carole Lombard, Humphrey Bogart and Lauren Bacall, and Spencer Tracy and Katharine Hepburn. Some of the classic films made during this period include *Gone with the Wind*, *King Kong*, *The Wizard of Oz*, and *Citizen Kane*.

Besides going to movies, Carol had a lot of other creative hobbies. She loved to read. One

of her favorite books was *The Yearling*, the story of a young boy who takes care of an orphaned fawn. In 1946, it was made into a movie, which Carol wanted to be first in line to see. Grimms' fairy tales also captured Carol's attention. She drew pencil sketches of fairy-tale scenes, bringing the stories to life. Sometimes Nanny would take Carol's drawings to her job at the movie studio. She'd leave the sketches behind in hopes that someone in the art department would "discover" Carol's art. But the employees there only left a note asking her not to use their art supplies!

Carol's other talent was music. Nanny was a trained musician who taught her to play the piano—although they couldn't afford one of their own. Carol's mother played the ukulele. Sometimes the three would gather round the kitchen table and sing in harmony together.

For a time, Carol thought she might want to be a cartoonist when she grew up. She even created her own comic strip, called "The Josephson Family," about a family whose names all began with the letter *J*. Carol's favorite newspaper comic strip was *Brenda Starr, Reporter*, about a red-haired newspaper reporter. Reading about Brenda's adventures inspired Carol to work on her junior high school newspaper.

One day, the paper assigned Carol to write about the school play. The tryouts were being held in the school auditorium. On a whim,

Carol decided to try out for the play herself. She wanted to play the part of a gum-chewing, wisecracking maid. But when Carol got up onstage to read her lines for the drama teacher, something strange happened. She looked out over the sea of faces staring up at her and . . . froze! Was this what stage fright felt like?

Carol stumbled through her reading, sure that she was not going to get the part. But the drama teacher must have seen something in her. The next day, Carol was surprised to learn that she was one of two finalists for the role. The drama teacher eventually decided to give the part to them both—Carol and a boy named Gordon. They would each play the role every other night. It wasn't the ideal solution, but it gave Carol her first taste of acting—and she liked it. The show-business bug had bitten her. Now she wanted to take it to the next level.

CHAPTER 2
Taking the Stage

When she completed junior high, Carol moved on to what she once called "the most famous high school in the whole wide world." Hollywood High was where movie stars sent their kids to prepare for college.

Hollywood High Liberal Arts Building

Even though she didn't have famous parents, Carol hoped to continue acting at her new school. Unfortunately, the teacher who ran the theater department retired just as Carol was starting tenth grade. For the next three years, there would be no school productions at Hollywood High. Carol ended up studying Spanish and art instead.

With no plays to appear in, Carol continued working for the school newspaper. She wrote her own column mixing humor and poetry. She was a straight-A student and began making plans to study journalism at the University of California at Los Angeles (UCLA). There was just one problem: She couldn't afford it.

In 1951, UCLA charged forty-two dollars a

year to attend. But the rent on Nanny's apartment was thirty-five dollars a month. There was not enough left over to pay Carol's tuition. Carol hoped that she would find the money somehow, but as the day to register for classes arrived, she still didn't have a plan. Then a stroke of good luck came her way.

One morning, Carol went out to check the mail. Inside the mailbox, she found an envelope with her name on it. When she opened it, a fifty-dollar bill came fluttering out. It was enough to cover tuition at UCLA for an entire year. But who had sent it?

Astonished, Carol checked the envelope for a return address. But there wasn't one. Whoever had sent this had delivered it by hand and left no note inside. Just one crisp bill with President Ulysses S. Grant's face on it. Carol pocketed the money and started making plans to register at UCLA that afternoon.

When she arrived on campus, another surprise awaited her: UCLA did not have a journalism department! So Carol would have to decide on a different subject to major in. She chose theater. In her heart, she believed acting was her true passion.

Carol (standing) in a play at UCLA

In the summer of 1951, Carol took a job as an usher at the Warner theater, a fancy "movie palace" on Hollywood Boulevard. Carol's job was to escort moviegoers to their seats. Carol loved the job because she could watch movies for free. But she didn't last long because she loved movies a little *too* much.

One night, the movie *Strangers on a Train* was

showing at the theater. Carol had seen it many times. When a couple arrived late for the start of the film, Carol instructed them to wait until the next showing. The movie was so good, she told them, it should be seen from beginning to end. But the theater manager overheard her and fired her on the spot. He felt she should have simply shown them to their seats, rather than ask them to wait. Carol was humiliated. She never forgot what it felt like to be fired.

Movie Palaces

Between 1910 and 1940, movie fans could watch their favorite films in style at one of America's many so-called "movie palaces." These grand theaters featured plush seats, huge chandeliers, air-conditioning, and velvet curtains that made them look and feel like royal palaces. They were built as luxurious spaces that would attract movie audiences. One of the most famous movie palaces was the Warner Bros. Hollywood Theatre, which opened in 1928. It seated 2,700 people and had a ceiling painted to look like the sky.

Movie palaces remained the best way to watch a movie until the 1950s, when they went out of fashion with the rise of television and modern "multiplex" movie theaters.

Warner Bros. Hollywood Theatre

Toward the end of her time in college, Carol started dating Don Saroyan, one of her fellow theater students. They dreamed of moving to New York City together after graduation to find work as actors on Broadway. But Carol didn't have the money to pay her way across the country.

And getting fired from her job at the movie theater hadn't helped.

One Saturday night in 1954, Carol and Don were performing together at a fancy Hollywood party. After acting out a scene from the Broadway musical *Annie Get Your Gun*, they were approached by one of the wealthy party guests. He told them how much he enjoyed their performance and asked what they planned to do after graduation. They told the man about their dream of moving to New York. He offered to help them. He told them to drop by his office on Monday morning. When Carol and Don arrived, the man had his accountant write two one-thousand-dollar checks—one for each of them. He instructed them to pay back the loan in five years, but he made them swear they would never reveal his identity. They agreed. And they never did.

Armed with enough cash to pay her way,

Carol started packing for her new life in New York City—and a date with the bright lights of Broadway.

CHAPTER 3
Climbing to the Top

Before Carol could leave for New York City, she got some bad news: Her father had died of pneumonia in a hospital in Los Angeles. He was only forty-seven years old.

Carol was saddened by her father's passing, but she remained determined to live out her show-business dream. Shortly before he died, she had promised that she would one day pay his way to New York to see her perform in her first show on Broadway. Now he would never get that chance.

Before she left California, Carol had one more promise to make. She told Nanny that if she ever got on television, she would send her grandmother a secret signal that only the two of them would understand. "I'll say hello by pulling on my left ear," Carol said. More than a year would pass before Carol made good on her promise.

In August 1954, Carol boarded a Greyhound bus headed east for New York City. She moved into the Rehearsal Club on West Fifty-Third Street, a residence for aspiring actresses. Her boyfriend, Don Saroyan, joined her in New York a few months later.

The Rehearsal Club

To pay her rent, Carol took a job as a hatcheck girl in a ladies' tearoom. Her job was to collect women's hats and coats and keep them in a coatroom while they ate. She was usually able to smuggle home some leftover food for herself and her friends. At night, Carol and Don would stroll down Broadway and gape at the bright neon lights on the theater marquees. "One day *my* name will be up there in lights," Carol declared. "Just wait and see."

Carol's early days in the big city were far from successful, however. She was turned down for many parts and had trouble finding an agent who would represent her. With her money running low, Carol came up with a brilliant idea: She and the other girls who lived at the Rehearsal Club would stage their own show, a musical revue, and invite every agent in town to come and watch them perform.

The Rehearsal Club Revue of 1955 turned out to be a smashing success. Carol's solo musical number earned rave reviews. After the show, twenty agents contacted her with offers. Arthur Willi, a

THE REHEARSAL CLUB

Presents

THE REHEARSAL CLUB REVUE

PRODUCED AND DIRECTED
BY
DON SAROYAN

ORIGINAL MUSIC
PETER DANIELS

ORIGINAL LYRICS
DICK ALLEN

ENSEMBLE CHOREOGRAPHY
MAYBIN HEWES

SETS AND LIGHTING
MING CHO LEE

theater veteran, promised Carol he could get her work on television.

It took a little time, but eventually Mr. Willi came through. He was able to land Carol a job on a network television show. There was just one catch: Her costar was made of wood. The male lead on *The Paul Winchell and Jerry Mahoney Show* was a ventriloquist's dummy named Jerry Mahoney. Carol's role would be to sing love songs to him. It wasn't the greatest job in the world, but it was better than no job at all. Carol eagerly accepted the gig.

On December 17, 1955, the same day Carol's first episode on *The Paul Winchell and Jerry Mahoney Show* was scheduled to debut, Carol and Don Saroyan were married by a justice of the peace in Yonkers, New York. That evening, she took the stage for the first time in front of a nationwide TV audience. True to her word, Carol bid hello to Nanny by tugging on her left earlobe as soon as she appeared on camera. Then she brought the house down by singing "Somewhere Over the Rainbow" to a wooden puppet.

Over the next few months, Carol became one of the most popular performers on the program. But even her talents couldn't save the show from being canceled by the network. Now that she had her first job in show business, however, there was no turning back. She got a supporting role on a TV sitcom, then a guest spot on a variety show. Eventually she was called to appear on legendary showman Ed Sullivan's Sunday night talent showcase.

Ed Sullivan (1901–1974)

Ed Sullivan was a legendary television host best known for his weekly variety show. *The Ed Sullivan Show* aired from 1948 to 1971. Sullivan's program, broadcast live every Sunday night, featured performances from up-and-coming acts like the Beatles, Elvis Presley, and the Supremes. He was known for his distinctive voice—he introduced every episode by promising a "really big shew"—and his ability to make stars out of unknown performers. The Ed Sullivan Theater on Broadway in New York City is named in his honor.

On January 6, 1957, Carol strode out onto the stage in front of a packed audience at Ed Sullivan's theater in Manhattan. The huge crowd was there to see another one of Sullivan's guests, a young rock 'n' roll sensation named Elvis Presley, but Carol didn't care that she wasn't the main attraction. Once again she tugged on her earlobe and launched into a song. Both the crowd in the theater and the audience watching from home loved her.

A couple of months later, Carol returned to California to visit her family. While she was there, her friends threw her a surprise party to congratulate her on her success. They presented her with a cake frosted with the words "60 million"—the number of people who had watched her appearance on *The Ed Sullivan Show*. While Carol was sure that most of those viewers had tuned in to see Elvis that night on TV and not her, she understood that a new phase of her show-business career was about to begin.

CHAPTER 4
Rising Star

The year 1957 had been a very good one for Carol. But 1958 started out on a sad note. That January, Carol's mother died after a short illness. She had been in poor health for quite some time because of her drinking.

To help her deal with the loss of her mother, Carol threw herself into her work. She made another appearance on *The Ed Sullivan Show* and performed her own nightclub act in Las Vegas.

But she still held out for her dream of starring on Broadway. In May 1959, that dream came true when she made her stage debut in a new musical called *Once Upon a Mattress*. A comedic version of the fairy tale "The Princess and the Pea," the show starred Carol in the lead role of Princess

Winnifred the Woebegone. Carol earned a Tony Award nomination for best actress in a musical. (The Tony Awards are given for achievements in American theater.) The show ran for over a year and has been revived many times since.

In the fall of 1959, she got an offer to join the cast of *The Garry Moore Show*, a TV variety hour featuring music and comedy skits. The show turned out to be a huge hit, earning Carol an

Emmy Award for her performance. (Emmys are awarded for excellence in the television industry.) Among the roles she played on the show was a messy cleaning woman, who would become one of her signature characters.

The weekly spot on *The Garry Moore Show* exposed Carol to millions of TV viewers nationwide. It also gave her a steady paycheck.

With a featured role on TV and a hit Broadway

show, Carol was flying high as 1959 came to a close. But all was not well at home. Her marriage to actor Don Saroyan was not a happy one. Don's own career had completely stalled. He resented the fact that Carol made so much more money than he did. After months of trying to work out their differences, the couple decided to get divorced.

Carol moved out of the cramped apartment they shared and into a luxury building overlooking New York's Central Park. While she waited for her divorce paperwork to go through the courts, she began dating Joe Hamilton, the producer of *The Garry Moore Show*. In May 1963, they were married. They had three children together, starting with daughter Carrie in December 1963. Carol also helped care for Joe's eight children from his previous marriage. It was quite a crowded household.

The 1960s were busy, happy years for Carol.

Carol Burnett with her family, 1970s

She continued to appear on *The Garry Moore Show* until it went off the air in 1964. She starred

in another Broadway musical, *Fade Out— Fade In*, but was forced to leave the show early after injuring her neck in a car accident. She starred in her own series of TV variety specials for the CBS network.

Perhaps most important of all, Carol was becoming friends with other female performers who shared her love of music and comedy. One of these was Julie Andrews, the English stage actress who won an Academy Award for playing Mary Poppins in the 1964 film. The pair made three TV specials together, beginning with 1962's *Julie and Carol at Carnegie Hall*. They have remained best friends ever since.

Carol Burnett and Julie Andrews

Another important friend and mentor was Lucille Ball, the television trailblazer and comedy legend. Lucy guest starred on one of Carol's highly successful CBS specials and invited her to appear on her own popular sitcom, *The Lucy*

Show. The two women remained close friends until Lucy's death in 1989. It was Lucy's example that inspired Carol to take the next important step in her career—and resulted in the creation of the iconic TV variety show that bears her name.

Carol Burnett on *The Lucy Show*

Lucille Ball (1911–1989)

Lucille Ball was a pioneering American actress, comedian, and television producer during the mid-twentieth century. She began her career as a model, went on to perform on Broadway, and eventually starred in films and on television. Best known for her starring role as Lucy Ricardo on the sitcom *I Love Lucy*, she was known for her zany physical comedy (using her whole body and her actions to be funny and to convey the joke to the audience). As the first woman to head a major television production  company, Desilu Productions, she blazed a trail for female performers like Mary Tyler Moore, Carol Burnett, and Tina Fey, among many others.

CHAPTER 5
The Carol Burnett Show

In 1967, Carol dealt with many changes. She and Joe had recently moved into a new house in Beverly Hills, a suburb of Los Angeles. In January of that year, she gave birth to their second child, a daughter named Jody Ann. The new house was much larger than their apartment in New York had been, and it allowed her to keep an eye on Nanny, who was elderly and living in a nursing home nearby.

Soon after Carol brought Jody home from the hospital, Nanny's health took a turn for the worse. She died in March 1967 at the age of eighty-one. The loss was devastating for Carol, who somehow found the strength to organize the funeral service while still taking care of her infant daughter. She made sure that Nanny was buried in a cemetery in Hollywood just steps from Nelson Eddy and Tyrone Power—two of her favorite movie stars from the 1940s. "She's got to love that," Carol thought.

That spring, Carol also had an important choice to make. The men who ran the CBS network offered her a show of her own, which would be called *Here's Agnes*. They envisioned a wacky sitcom in the style of *I Love Lucy*. This would have given Carol the chance to star in her own weekly series. There was just one problem: Carol had no interest in doing a sitcom. She felt her strength was mixing music and comedy in the variety format, like she had been doing on *The Garry Moore Show*.

Carol met with the CBS executives and told them about her idea for a show: an hour-long variety series with guest stars, comedy sketches, and music. Carol would host, just as Ed Sullivan had done on his show. But CBS didn't like the idea. "Comedy-variety shows are traditionally hosted by men," one of the executives told her. "It's really not for a gal."

Carol thought the time was right to change

the traditional way of doing things. After all, no woman had starred in her own TV show until Lucille Ball broke down that barrier. But how could she convince CBS to give her the chance to break this one?

Luckily for Carol, there was a clause (a specially worded part of the document) in her contract with the network that let her choose her next project. In fact, she had five years from the date *The Garry Moore Show* ended to decide what kind of show she wanted to make. Though CBS tried to talk her out of it, Carol stuck to her original idea, just as Lucy would have. The network agreed to give her the variety hour she wanted.

The Carol Burnett Show was scheduled to debut in September 1967. Now Carol just had to hire a cast and crew to get the show off the ground. Working with her husband, Joe, who served as producer, Carol began hiring writers and guest stars.

Lucille Ball was one of the first stars to agree to appear on the show, but the regular cast took some time to come together.

Carol needed an experienced comic actor to appear alongside her in the skits. She found the perfect comedy costar in Harvey Korman, who had been on *The Danny Kaye Show*. Korman could play any role, from an elderly grandmother to the president of the United States. For the romantic "leading man" parts, Carol selected ruggedly handsome Lyle Waggoner. And for the supporting female roles, she turned to an up-and-coming performer named Vicki Lawrence. Like Carol, Vicki had a musical as well as a comedy background. Best of all, she looked a lot like Carol, making it easy for her to play Carol's sister in many of the sketches.

Viva Variety

The 1950s and '60s were a golden era for television variety shows. Hosts like Jackie Gleason, Sid Caesar, and Milton Berle specialized in comedy sketches, while Lawrence Welk, Ed Sullivan, and Dean Martin mixed in musical guests and novelty acts like jugglers, puppeteers, and circus performers. Because the performers were always different, audiences tuned in week after week to find out which types of acts the host would showcase.

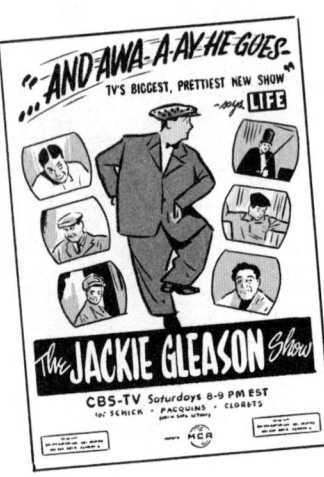

Although variety-show programming went out of fashion in the 1980s, modern shows like *Saturday Night Live* still carry on in the spirit of these early pioneers.

As the debut of her show approached, Carol was filled with anticipation. "I'm Nellie Nerves," she told an interviewer. Although Carol had plenty of show-business experience, she had never starred in her own weekly series. She worried about how she would do at introducing guests and talking to the audience.

Her fears were unfounded. *The Carol Burnett Show* was an instant hit with audiences and critics. Carol won special praise for her role as host. She treated the live audience to her famed "Tarzan yell," which she had been doing since childhood,

and remembered to tug on her earlobe at the close of every show in her private message to Nanny, who she believed would always be watching over her.

But it was the recurring comedy sketches that truly won viewers over. Playing off of Carol's love of old movies, there were skits that made fun of classic films (*Went with the Wind!* instead of *Gone with the Wind,* for example). Her love of TV soap operas inspired a spoof called *As the Stomach Turns.* And the entire cast appeared in a regular sketch called "The Family," about a loud Texas couple named Eunice and Ed and their unwelcome houseguest: Eunice's elderly "Mama." Carol even revived her popular cleaning woman character from *The Garry Moore Show.*

Joining the cast on a regular basis was comic actor Tim Conway, a friend of Harvey Korman, whose antics often made him crack up with laughter on the air. Carol's husband, Joe Hamilton, wrote the show's theme song, "I'm So Glad We Had This Time Together," which became known as "Carol's Theme." And as the show grew more and more successful, big-name guest stars lined up to get in on the fun. In addition to Lucille Ball, Rock Hudson, Cher, Betty White, and Rita Moreno all appeared multiple times.

Almost overnight, it seemed, Carol Burnett had changed the face of television and her own career. She proved that a woman could host a variety show, build an all-star cast, and earn herself millions of new fans. The only question left was, What would she do with her newfound fame? The world would soon find out.

CHAPTER 6
Carol Burnett, Superstar

The Carol Burnett Show was a hit. Its star was now one of the most famous women in America. And she was being honored for her work. Carol's college, UCLA, named her its "Alumna of the Year" for 1968. She was the first woman ever to receive this honor. The Hasty Pudding Society,

Carol Burnett accepting the Woman of the Year Award
from the Hasty Pudding Society

a club at Harvard University, selected her as its Woman of the Year. Carol flew to Boston to accept the award in person.

In the summer of 1968, Carol gave birth to Erin Kate, her third daughter with husband Joe Hamilton. With *The Carol Burnett Show* renewed for another season, Carol and Joe began

to enjoy their success. They bought a house on the ocean in Malibu Beach, California. The vast mansion had an Olympic-size swimming pool big enough for their large family to splash around in. They also bought an old-time Ford Model A car, which they painted green and named "Mavis" after Joe's mother.

Although she was now a superstar, Carol herself hadn't changed much. When she wasn't performing, she was helping Joe with the kids or relaxing at home in front of the television. Carol was a night owl, and she still loved old movies. Sometimes she would stay up all night watching two or three classic films in a row. Some of these movies, like *Sunset Boulevard* starring Gloria Swanson, provided the inspiration for new skits on her show.

In the summer of 1969, Carol noticed a sharp pain in her right foot. A doctor diagnosed her with Morton's toe, a painful condition that usually affects athletes. Perhaps all the physical comedy Carol had performed onstage all those years had finally taken its toll. Carol needed surgery and had to walk on crutches for several weeks. Luckily, her foot healed just in time for her to start taping the third season of *The Carol Burnett Show*. Nothing, it seemed, could slow her down.

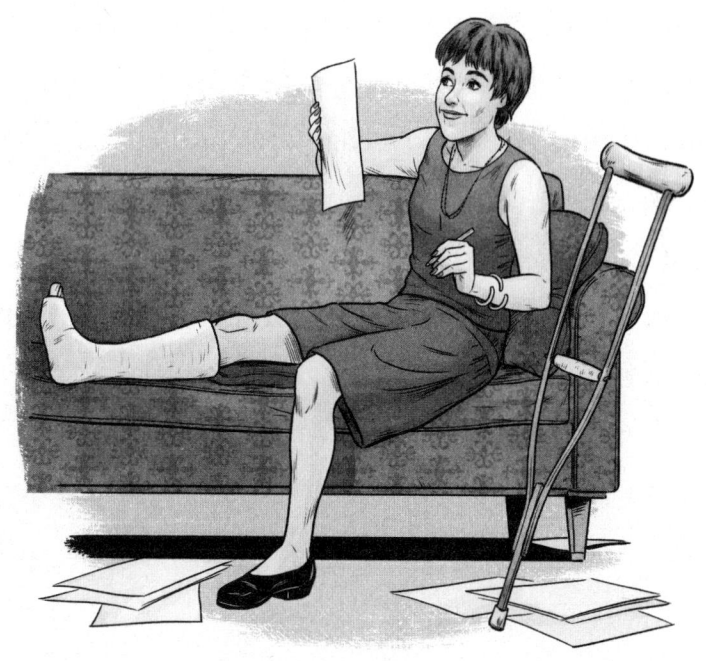

On November 10, 1969, Carol became the first celebrity guest to appear on a brand-new children's television show called *Sesame Street*. A mix of music, comedy, cartoons, and educational fun, *Sesame Street* would go on to become a worldwide sensation. In two brief sketches on the show's first episode, Carol showed the Muppets how to wiggle your nose and then she kissed a rubber ducky.

As the 1970s dawned, Carol began to feel like branching out. Her TV show was still successful, but she believed she had more to offer in the fields of music, movies, and perhaps even a return to Broadway. She started by recording a series of albums featuring musical duets with other stars, such as her friend Julie Andrews. Then, in July 1972, she starred in a TV version of her Broadway hit *Once Upon a Mattress* for CBS.

One day, while she was rehearsing for *Once Upon a Mattress*, Carol got a call from an old friend, actor Walter Matthau.

Once Upon a Mattress

Sesame Street

Sesame Street is a groundbreaking children's television program that debuted on November 10, 1969. Set in front of a large home at 123 Sesame Street in New York City, the show combines live-action and animation with Muppet characters like Big Bird, Oscar the Grouch, and Cookie Monster. *Sesame Street* pioneered preschool educational television by teaching young children about numbers and letters using fast-paced sketches and catchy songs.

Over the years, many celebrity guest stars have dropped by "the Street" to share songs and stories with the Muppets.

He recommended Carol for a part in a romantic comedy he was making called *Pete 'n' Tillie*. It was her first starring role in a Hollywood movie. Carol was nervous but eager to show what she could do.

Pete 'n' Tillie follows the romance between two oddball characters: Tillie  Schlaine, played by Carol, and Pete Seltzer, played by Walter Matthau. The film features many scenes of zany physical comedy but also many dramatic scenes that allowed Carol to demonstrate that she was able to play a dramatic character as well. Critics praised Carol's performance. She was rewarded with a Golden Globe nomination for best actress. Two years later, she costarred with Matthau again in another film comedy, *The Front Page*.

On May 21, 1975, Carol was honored
with a star on the Hollywood Walk of Fame, a
sidewalk in Los Angeles where celebrities from
movies and TV shows—and even some famous
animals—have their names inscribed on star-
shaped plaques that are placed into the pavement.
When she was asked to choose the site of her
star, Carol selected 6439 Hollywood Boulevard,
right in front of the old Warner Bros. movie

theater where she had been fired from her job as an usher back in 1951.

Around this time, Carol began to think about life after *The Carol Burnett Show*. By 1977, the show had been on for ten years. It was still winning awards and attracting large audiences. But Carol thought it wasn't as fresh and funny as it once had been. Maybe the writers were running out of ideas? Or maybe Carol was just tired of doing a weekly series and wanted to try something new.

Emmy Awards Show, 1972

In the summer of 1977, Harvey Korman announced he was leaving the cast to star in his own TV series on ABC. His replacement, Dick Van Dyke, left after only three months. By the end of the year, Carol decided that it was time to end the show. She took the remaining cast members to dinner and announced her decision.

"I just feel that eleven years is enough," she said as she started to cry.

On March 17, 1978, Carol and the cast taped the final episode of *The Carol Burnett Show*. The two-hour special included clips from some of the show's funniest sketches. When it was over, Carol came out onstage to say farewell to the live audience. She thanked the cast and crew, tugged on her earlobe one last time, and sang one last chorus of her theme song:

I'm so glad we had this time together.

CHAPTER 7
A New Beginning

The Carol Burnett Show was over, but Carol Burnett was far from finished. Her show had made her one of the highest-paid women in America.

While it was on the air, she had earned more than $100 million a year. Now she wanted to keep busy, making movies and TV specials.

Carol and Joe bought a new house in Beverly Hills that cost $2 million. It had two tennis courts and a large Olympic-size swimming pool. Carol also bought a house for her half sister, Chrissie, who was now divorced and raising a child on her own.

But with Carol's fame and fortune came new dangers as well. People trespassed at her home, as if Carol wouldn't mind. One time an entire family from Ohio showed up in Carol and Joe's kitchen and waited for them to come down for breakfast. They even looked inside the kitchen cabinets.

To help her deal with the stress, Carol tried to keep her mind and body fit. To relax, she started meditating, an ancient practice of emptying your mind. She took classes in yoga, an exercise to stretch muscles and breathe deeply.

And she completely changed her diet. She stopped eating junk food and started eating more fruits, vegetables, and other healthy foods.

Some of Carol's friends urged her to continue doing comedy. But Carol wanted to expand her roles into more dramatic ones. Shortly after *The Carol Burnett Show* went off the air, she accepted a part in a television movie called *Friendly Fire*. It told the true story of the mother of a soldier who had been killed during the Vietnam War.

Carol had to audition against a lot of talented actresses for the role. At first, she wasn't sure she could handle such a challenging part. But the writer and director of *Friendly Fire* had faith in her. They thought Carol's sweet and wholesome image made her perfect for the picture—and they were right. *Friendly Fire* aired on television on April 22, 1979. More than sixty million people tuned in to watch. Critics praised Carol's performance as Iowa mom Peg Mullen.

A scene from *Friendly Fire*

"The best thing she's ever done," raved Carol's husband, Joe. *Friendly Fire* won four Emmy Awards.

For her next major role, Carol returned to familiar territory. She played the part of Miss Hannigan, the villainous orphanage manager, in the movie version of the hit Broadway musical *Annie*. Miss Hannigan was just the sort of over-the-top character Carol used to play on her own show. She enjoyed wearing the outlandish costumes and performed in several musical numbers. It was a refreshing change after the heavy drama of *Friendly Fire*.

Carol Burnett as Miss Hannigan in *Annie*

Carol also plunged herself into new television projects. In 1983, she helped launch *Mama's Family*, a TV sitcom based on a popular sketch from *The Carol Burnett Show*. Carol played Eunice, the feisty daughter of Vicki Lawrence's Mama character.

Harvey Korman also guest starred on the show, which went on to run for six seasons and 130 episodes.

That same year, Carol got to live out a lifelong dream when she was cast in a small role on her favorite soap opera, *All My Children*. Carol had been a fan of the show since she was a child. She loved the dramatic situations and colorful characters who populated the world of daytime drama. On *All My Children*, she played

Verla Grubbs, the long-lost daughter of con man Langley Wallingford. Carol appeared on the show several times over the following years. And Verla Grubbs became a fan-favorite character.

Carol Burnett as Verla Grubbs in *All My Children*

Daytime Drama

Daytime dramas, or "serials," started on radio in the 1920s. They featured highly dramatic situations and were designed to appeal to female listeners. In those early days, many daytime dramas were sponsored by soap and detergent companies, so they came to be known as "soap operas."

In the late 1940s and into the 1950s, soap operas began to appear on the new medium of television. *The Guiding Light*, *As the World Turns*, and *General Hospital* were just a few of the series that began their long TV runs during this period. In recent years, the popularity of daytime soap operas has declined, but three still remain on-air: *The Bold and the Beautiful*, *General Hospital*, and *The Young and the Restless*.

CHAPTER 8
Tough Times

In the 1980s, Carol experienced a series of personal difficulties. It all started when the *National Enquirer* published a story suggesting

that Carol was seen acting disorderly in a Washington, DC, restaurant. Carol denied their version of the story. To protect her reputation, Carol filed a lawsuit against the *National Enquirer*. She won and was awarded $800,000 in damages. But the trial took a toll on her. She felt like her personal life was being exposed for all the world to see.

Around this same time, Carol's teenage daughter Carrie began having trouble at school. Her personality started to change. Once, she had been a happy, smiling child. Now, she seemed angry and disagreeable. Carol and Joe began to suspect she was using drugs. As it turned out, they were right. Carrie had started smoking marijuana at age thirteen. She had also developed a dependence on alcohol.

The family doctor suggested that Carrie might benefit from entering a drug rehab center. There she would follow a strict program based on the methods of Alcoholics Anonymous (AA). At first, Carrie resisted this idea. She even tried running away from home. But Carol and Joe insisted. They checked her in to the Palmer Drug Abuse Program in Houston, Texas.

Alcoholics Anonymous

Alcoholics Anonymous, often called simply "AA," was founded in the 1930s by a man named Bill W. and his friend Dr. Bob S. They realized they needed help to stop drinking because it was too difficult a task for them to do alone. They created AA to help others who needed this same kind of help.

In AA, people come together in meetings to talk about their struggles with alcohol and to support one another. They share their stories and listen to one another. They also follow a special program called the "Twelve Steps" to help them stay sober and make better life choices. And they remain anonymous by never sharing with others what is heard at AA meetings.

Carrie finally got sober when she was seventeen years old. She became an advocate for other teens trying to cope with drug addiction. Once bitter enemies, she and her mother became best friends again. Carol and Carrie even traveled to Moscow together to help introduce the first Alcoholics Anonymous branch in the Soviet Union.

Their child's struggle took a toll on Carol and Joe's relationship—and Joe's health. On New Year's Eve in 1981, Joe had a heart attack while attending a wedding in Los Angeles. After Carol helped him recover his health, the couple decided to separate. Carol believed that the stress of dealing with their daughter's addiction had driven them apart. They eventually agreed to get a divorce. But they stayed close friends.

While Joe remained in Los Angeles, Carol settled into a home they had bought in Hawaii.

She could still fly back and forth to Hollywood when she needed to work, which she did often. In the fall of 1982, Carol starred in a new TV movie, *Life of the Party: The Story of Beatrice*. The film told the life story of Beatrice O'Reilly, a former alcoholic who founded Los Angeles's first rehab center for women.

Carol took the part because of her recent experience with Carrie—and because Beatrice reminded her of her own mother. "She was a trailblazer," Carol said. "Thirty years ago it was very unusual to see a woman at an AA meeting." To prepare for the part, Carol met and spent time with the real Beatrice O'Reilly. They ended up becoming close friends. Carol even said that Beatrice was what her mother would have been like if she had stayed sober.

Carol's portrayal of Beatrice O'Reilly won praise from critics and viewers. The movie was proof that even in these tough personal times, she could still deliver a great performance.

CHAPTER 9
Living Legend

Throughout the 1980s, Carol remained active in television. She also devoted more of her time to writing. In 1986, she published a book. Titled *One More Time*, it tells the story of her life and career. It became a national best seller.

Around this time, Carol's daughter Carrie started to pursue her own acting career. Carol and Carrie did interviews together where they discussed Carol's book, their shared love of show business, and Carrie's struggle with addiction.

The two even worked together on a play, *Hollywood Arms*, based on Carol's childhood.

In the following decade, Carol won another Emmy Award—her sixth—for playing the mother of main character Jamie Buchman on the TV sitcom *Mad About You*.

In 1995, thirty years after her last Broadway show, she returned to Broadway in the comedy *Moon Over Buffalo*. She was nominated for a Tony Award. Four years later, she appeared in another Broadway musical, *Putting It Together*.

The cast of *Mad About You*

Around that time, Carol starred in a musical in Long Beach, California. While there she met Brian Miller, the drummer in the show's orchestra. The two became friends and soon started dating. They married in November 2001.

Not long after the wedding, Carol was struck by another terrible loss. Carrie had been diagnosed with lung cancer. She died in January 2002 at the age of thirty-eight. To honor her daughter's memory, Carol founded the Carrie Hamilton Theatre in Pasadena, California.

Carol Burnett with Martha Williamson,
member of the board of the Pasadena Playhouse,
at the opening of the Carrie Hamilton Theatre

Carol turned seventy-five in 2008. And she was still performing regularly. In 2009, she received a special tribute when one of her costumes from

The Carol Burnett Show was added to the collection of the Smithsonian National Museum of American History in Washington, DC. The dress that was chosen was the one she wore as "Miss Starlett" in the 1976 *Gone with the Wind* spoof *Went with the Wind!*—one that had been made from the curtains hung in Miss Starlett's mansion windows.

In 2013, Carol was awarded the Mark Twain Prize for American Humor. Many of her friends and costars showed up at the awards ceremony to pay tribute to her. Julie Andrews and Tim Conway were there, as were many of the female performers who had been inspired by her, including Tina Fey, Amy Poehler, and Maya Rudolph.

The Mark Twain Prize

The Mark Twain Prize for American Humor is an award that honors outstanding comedians, writers, and entertainers. It was established in 1998 and named after Mark Twain (1835–1910), a famous American author known for his witty and clever stories. The prize ceremony takes place every year in Washington, DC. Tina Fey, Whoopi Goldberg, and Julia Louis-Dreyfus are among the notable female winners of the Mark Twain Prize.

In 2017, CBS aired *The Carol Burnett Show: 50th Anniversary Special,* an all-star tribute to the show. Vicki Lawrence and Lyle Waggoner returned from the original cast to share clips from the series that had made them famous.

Before the special aired, Carol spoke to the press about her role as a female trailblazer. "They said it was a man's game . . . ," she said of hosting her own variety show, "because it hadn't been done. But that doesn't mean it couldn't be done."

In 2018, the Golden Globes created a special award in Carol's name. The Carol Burnett Award honors excellence in television. Actor Steve Carell presented the first award to Carol herself in 2019. Ellen DeGeneres, Norman Lear, and Ryan Murphy have all won the award in recent years.

Even as she received the recognition and awards, Carol continued working well into her late eighties. In 2019, she provided the voice of a talking chair named Chairol Burnett in the animated movie *Toy Story 4*.

Chairol Burnett in *Toy Story 4*

In July and August 2022, she guest starred on four episodes of the TV drama series *Better Call Saul*.

When she reached her ninetieth birthday, Carol didn't want to just blow out some candles. She wanted to stage a full-on variety show surrounded by friends, fans, and fellow performers. On April 26, 2023, the star-studded two-hour TV special *Carol Burnett: 90 Years of Laughter + Love* aired on NBC.

Julie Andrews, Vicki Lawrence, Lily Tomlin, Steve Carell, Amy Poehler, Ellen DeGeneres, Bob Odenkirk, and Cher were among the celebrities who gathered to celebrate Carol's long life and career, in what was hailed as one of the greatest birthday parties of all time.

At the end of the special, pop star Katy Perry handed Carol the microphone to sing the final verse of the famed theme song from *The Carol Burnett Show*, "I'm So Glad We Had This Time Together." Was Carol saying "so long" to her audience for the last time? No one in the crowd wanted to believe that could be true.

After nearly seventy years of making America laugh, Carol ended her show with a tear in her eye. The many millions she has entertained, inspired, and blazed a trail for over the years can only hope there will be more good times to come.

Timeline of Carol Burnett's Life

1933 — Carol Creighton Burnett is born in San Antonio, Texas

1940 — Moves to Hollywood, California

1951 — Enrolls at the University of California, Los Angeles (UCLA)

1954 — Moves to New York City

1958 — Mother, Ina, dies

1959 — Stars on Broadway in *Once Upon a Mattress*

— Joins the cast of *The Garry Moore Show*

1960 — Nominated for a Tony Award for *Once Upon a Mattress*

1962 — Wins her first Emmy Award for *The Garry Moore Show*

1967 — Grandmother Mabel "Mae" Eudora White dies

— *The Carol Burnett Show* debuts

1972 — Stars in feature film *Pete 'n' Tillie*

1978 — *The Carol Burnett Show* ends

1979 — Stars in the TV movie *Friendly Fire*

1986 — Publishes her memoir *One More Time*

2002 — Daughter Carrie Hamilton dies

2005 — Receives the Presidential Medal of Freedom

2013 — Awarded the Mark Twain Prize for American Humor

2019 — Receives the first Carol Burnett Award, a special Golden Globe Award, which is named for her

2023 — Celebrates her ninetieth birthday

Timeline of the World

1933 — The first drive-in movie theater opens in Pennsauken, New Jersey

1945 — The United Nations is founded to foster peace among nations

1950 — North Korea invades South Korea, starting the three-year Korean War

1969 — The Woodstock music festival, billed as "three days of peace and music," is held in Bethel, New York

1990 — Hubble Space Telescope is launched by NASA and the European Space Agency

2001 — September 11 terrorist attacks kill almost three thousand people in New York City; Washington, DC; and Shanksville, Pennsylvania

2005 — The YouTube app is officially launched on December 15, serving over two million video views a day

2008 — Barack Obama is elected the first African American president of the United States

2013 — American scientists use a 3D printer to create a living, lab-grown human ear

2023 — Charles III is crowned king of the United Kingdom following the death of his mother, Queen Elizabeth II, in 2022

Bibliography

Burnett, Carol. *Carrie and Me: A Mother-Daughter Love Story*. New York: Simon & Schuster, 2013.

Burnett, Carol. *In Such Good Company: Eleven Years of Laughter, Mayhem, and Fun in the Sandbox*. New York: Crown Archetype, 2016.

Burnett, Carol. *One More Time: A Memoir*. New York: Random House, 2003.

Burnett, Carol. *This Time Together: Laughter and Reflection*. New York: Three Rivers Press, 2010.

Burnett, Carol. *What I Want to Be When I Grow Up*. New York: Simon & Schuster, 1975.

Taraborrelli, J. Randy. *Laughing Till It Hurts: The Complete Life and Career of Carol Burnett*. New York: William Morrow & Co., 1988.